# HAPPIER THINKING

By Lana Grace Riva

# Hello

I am not the happiest person. I don't always have a smile on my face. I don't wake up feeling full of joy each morning, racing to get out of bed, high fiving the wall. (Do people high five walls? It seems like something a super happy person might do. Maybe.). I am much more likely to stumble over something on the floor and grace the day with a curse as my first word.

Aside from occasional low moods that most of us experience at some point, I have suffered more seriously with bouts of depression where I've felt like I was drowning in darkness. Unable to even contemplate getting out of bed let alone lifting my arm to high five anything.

Ok... so... erm... 'why are you writing this book?? I want to know how to be happy!' you are probably thinking. Sure, I am not a trained professional in psychology able to impart years of research and wisdom on the subject of happiness, but what I can do is share with you some things that have really helped me lift my mood and think happier.

I have read a lot about mental health, I've attended mindfulness classes, I've been to therapy, I've tried to educate myself in general on how the brain works. All in a bid to help myself stay afloat in life. Throughout all that I began writing down what I realized was working for me - mainly because I have a terrible memory, but also because I knew I'd find it helpful to have it all collected in one place. So it occurred to me that as I was writing it down anyway... I should write it in book form and share it with you lovely people in case it may be of use to others.

It's quite a short book, partly because it's easier to remember the content that way. Mainly though, it's because if you are impatient like me about seeing results you will want to just get on with putting into practice what I've written about, as opposed to spending vast amounts of time reading about theory.

I won't be going into scientific detail about parts of the brain, using exciting terms such as cortex and amygdala. Reading about those I found truly fascinating, but the main take away from my reading there which is relevant here is that it is entirely possible to change how you think.

You may feel as I have in the past that 'this is how I think so I'm stuck thinking this way forever', 'I'm always going to react this way', 'I'm always going to be unhappy', 'I must have just been born a negative thinker'. The good news is that these statements are not true, you are not stuck with your current brain, it is ever evolving and within your control to change. Well, unless the medical professionals in the books I read were misleading me... in which case... er... But in all seriousness, I've seen it in myself. I can definitely notice a difference in how I think, I feel like I am re-training my brain so it's absolutely possible for you to do the same.

If you consider yourself already generally quite a happy person that is wonderful. Hearing that others are happy is actually one thing that makes me happy so thank you for existing. If you are such a person, you are probably unlikely to be reading this book but in case you are – I'm sure there is always room for improvement, or you could be hoping to help others become happier. This book is not aimed at any specific type of person. All levels of current happiness welcome.

I must warn you at this point that what is within this book is not an overnight fix for instant happiness. I imagine I would be forever famous if that were the case. I have no wish to be forever famous. Not that becoming famous would stop me from sharing such an amazing fix if I had it. But I don't. So I'll stop talking about the imaginary fix now since well... it's imaginary.

Instead I am presenting you with suggestions that require some work and practice on your part. If you are willing to put in some time and effort I think you will be pleased you did and will be rewarded with happier thinking.

Don't worry though, I am not going to set homework exercises in each chapter that will be marked and assessed at later stages. That might work for some but for others it can end up making you feel worse if you don't manage to do the homework. I am not here to make you feel guilty or like a failure for not following exact advice so I'm not going to outline any specific structure to this. There is no competition for who can achieve the most happy thoughts. It really is up to you how much effort and practice you put in and how much time you want to dedicate to the suggestions.

Yes, it's probably like the good old cliché tells us – the more effort you put in, the more benefit you get out. I would argue though that whilst that may be true, even if you only occasionally remember about one of the suggestions and it makes you feel happier then it has been a worthwhile read. More happy thinking is better than less happy thinking, even if only by one happy thought.

Each chapter offers a suggestion for you to try out to make your thinking happier. Some overlap a little and are in a similar vein, but I've split them up to try and be more helpful and reinforce principals (rather than to simply annoy you with repetition...).

I would urge you to try out all of them and practice each for a while before assessing whether it's something that's going to work for you long term. If it helps you to allocate a certain amount of time to each then do so. I would advise though not to give up on one too quickly if it doesn't work for you straight away. Remember my earlier ramblings about the overnight imaginary fix?

Keep in mind that you are essentially re-training your brain to think a different way. Training in most things in life takes many more than just one attempt, and this is no different.

Ok let's get started...

# Don't write off the day

The first actions of the day. You wake up when the alarm goes off, but it feels like it's surely still the middle of the night. Didn't you only just fall asleep? It's dark outside, maybe the alarm is wrong. Maybe you're dreaming. You remember it's winter. That means darkness in the morning. (Yes ok, that last sentence is not applicable to those living in parts of the world where it's light in the morning but let's just assume for the purposes of this scenario...).

Aaargh, the alarm is still going... the alarm has never randomly gone off at the wrong time before in the middle of the night so probably doubtful it's doing that now. Hard to dispute that all signs are likely pointing to time to get up.

You get in the shower and realize the shampoo bottle is empty, but you've already gone under the water so have to scramble about the bathroom dripping water everywhere trying to find the new bottle. Did you even buy a new bottle? It was out of stock when you had last thought to buy some.

You get dressed but what you planned to wear has a tear in it or a stain on it you hadn't realized was there. Maybe it's actually in the laundry basket because you wore it a few days ago. What else can you wear? You're going to be late for work.

You go to make breakfast and the milk bottle has a particularly well secured on lid. Great for transporting it from the shops to your home. Not so great for your need to make a quick breakfast. In your struggle to free the lid the milk spills all over the floor. Lovely. Yep, you're really going to be late for work.

When these types of things happen at the start of the day how often do you find yourself saying 'well, this is obviously going to be a bad day...'. Your mindset is now in negative mode.

When someone asks you how you are, your reply will more than likely be formed based on your morning experience - 'oh, I'm having a bad day today', 'I'm having one of those days...', 'I must have got out the wrong side of the bed'. (I never understand that last one - what makes one side of the bed wrong? I guess if it was up against the wall but then it would be impossible to get out of so wouldn't apply. Anyway...you get the point...).

Your mind has started on the negative path, so you will be more aware of further bad things you can pin on the 'bad day'. Each day is filled with good and bad but on these so called 'bad days' you will invariably notice mostly, if not only, the bad.

The next time you catch yourself labelling a day as bad, stop and challenge this thought that the whole day is tainted.

Try and peel that label off and apply it instead to only the particular part that has been perceived as bad. Your shower experience was bad. Your breakfast making experience was bad. Your getting dressed experience was bad. The day holds many more experiences. They all have the equal potential to be good or bad but pre-labelling them discounts that potential.

Make a special effort to look out for good things instead of further bad ones so you can prove this. If you really pay attention to all events that happen in a day you will see there is always some good present. If you have written off the day as bad you have effectively closed off your mind to noticing any good. Practice making a conscious choice to believe the day holds many opportunities for good and bad and shift your focus to paying attention to the good.

Happier thinking involves opening your awareness up to noticing good things at all times. They are not on a schedule, nor do they immediately disappear from the day if the day starts off with a bad experience.

Keep reminding yourself that there is always the possibility of good appearing no matter the time, no matter the day, no matter what has gone before it. So don't write off the day along with the possibility of noticing any good.

By Lana Grace Riva

# Turn negatives into positives

Consider a scenario of meeting up with a friend for lunch and the following happens:

Your friend is fifteen minutes late.

The waiter is slow to take your order.

The food arrives and is not what you ordered.

Consider each of these occurrences in turn and think about any possible good that may have actually been caused by them. For example:

Your friend being late allows you time to quickly catch up on a few emails.

The waiter taking a long time meant you could spend more time catching up with your friend.

The food tastes delicious despite not being what you had ordered.

It often comes more naturally to think negatively about experiences like the above. When something not so great happens, your mind views it only as negative signaling to you to feel unhappy. You can change this natural instinct though by practicing looking for positives.

Your mind may just stop after the initial three thoughts above and you almost resign yourself to accepting that the experience overall is bad. But what you can try instead is thinking more about each one and looking for a positive as shown in the second set of thoughts.

Think about a recent experience you've had which you felt went badly. For example – a visit to the shops, a night out, a phone call with a friend, a work meeting.

Now try and apply the same thought process as the lunch example above to think of good things that actually arose out of anything you perceived as bad. Practicing this each time you have a bad experience will help it become more natural to take a positive view. Let's look at another example.

You go shopping to buy groceries.

They've run out of the biscuits you normally buy.

There's bad traffic.

You get home and realize you forgot to buy something.

Now let's embark on some positive searching to find possible good that might have arisen:

You couldn't get your biscuits, but it gave you the opportunity to try something new and perhaps discover a new biscuit you like.

The traffic being bad might have meant the shops were quieter by the time you got there.

You find you still actually have some left of the thing you forgot to buy. Or you realize it's not actually essential and you can easily go without it until your next trip to the shops.

Now, just to be clear, these are purely examples and will obviously not apply in their exact form to every restaurant/shopping experience you have. But they can be adapted for the same positive outcomes.

You might be thinking 'what if the waiter gets my order wrong AND I then hate what they bring me instead?!' Yes, this is entirely possible. And annoying. The point is to try and assess the situation as a whole and really search out the positive side effects of any bad occurrences. And keep searching.

For example – the waiter gets your order wrong, the food they bring you instead you hate... but... they swap it for you and give you your meal free. Or your friend swaps their meal with yours. Or the whole food part of the meal may well just be a complete disaster, but you still enjoy the company of your friend.

If it helps you could view it as a challenge to keep going until you can think of one positive, even if it's only one small thing.

Happier thinking involves searching out and seeing the good in things. Even those things that initially seem only bad. If you look hard enough, there will be something good lurking around somewhere. Who doesn't love a treasure hunt.

# Journal good things

At the end of each day we often reflect on things that happened during the day and can sometimes get caught ruminating over something bad.

'Why did I behave that way?'

'Why didn't I prepare better for that situation to alter the outcome?'

'Why didn't I say this to that person?'

'Why did that happen to me?'

We learn from mistakes so this thinking is not completely unhelpful, but it turns unhelpful if we continue to repetitively go over and over it.

It is as though we are almost expecting a different outcome if we can just keep thinking about it hard enough. Well sure... good luck with that... try as you might, the day's events are in the past and you have zero control over altering them. Our brains don't seem to always get that memo though and they won't stop going over and over things causing unhappy thinking.

A tip to breaking the unhelpful cycle of negative rumination is to journal good things.

Think back over the day and think of some good things that happened. The purpose of this is to switch direction of your thinking - by the end of the exercise you will likely have pulled yourself away from the negative ruminating road and set yourself onto a happier good thinking road.

You could do this just in your mind but it's usually more effective written down, so you can keep a record. Even those with the greatest of memories I'm sure would struggle to remember the good things they thought of weeks/months ago (if you succeed in that then please do share your advice on how to gain such an amazing memory).

Do this exercise regularly (ideally daily but choose what works for you). Regular practice will make it easier to naturally become more and more aware of good things over time. The other benefit of this is you will be creating a book (amazing memory people aside) of reminders of good things that you can refer back to in times when you are struggling with feeling negative.

You may find it difficult at first to think of good things but keep in mind they don't need to be big things. Some examples to help you are below:

- Enjoying a meal. You could narrow it down to specifics – you discover a new ingredient you like, you enjoyed preparing the meal, you found a time saving meal preparation technique, you discovered a new recipe, the meal itself tasted really good.

- A nice conversation with a friend – they may have given you a good piece of advice, shared with you some good news, paid you a compliment, recommended a good tv show.

- Discovering a good book – one you've started to read, one that's just been released by an author you really like, one someone has recommended to you which you can look forward to reading in future.

- Hearing a good song – discovering a new one you like, hearing an old favorite, hearing one that reminds you of a happy memory.

- A delivery arrives on time – perhaps it arrived even earlier than you expected, it arrives undamaged, it arrives as you expected so there will be no need to return it.

- Finding something you thought was lost – or even something you hadn't realized you'd lost – perhaps a stranger hands you back something you dropped.

- Waking up before your alarm – you may wake up feeling alert and like you had a good night sleep, you may remember a nice dream, your room might be a nice temperature to wake up to.

You can keep them general or be more specific and detailed, it's up to you, however, if you are more detailed it will be easier to think of new things each day. Also, thinking more in detail makes it easier to dwell on good which will be discussed in a later chapter.

There are no set rules though. Noting the same good thing on more than one day is perfectly acceptable. A good thing happening twice is just as good as two different good things happening really isn't it.

Happier thinking is easier if you remember about the good things, so journaling is a good habit that facilitates this.

# Much you can't control but your reactions you can

The boiler is broken. Again. 'Aaarrrggghhh. This is so annoying! It will never be fixed.'

This is an inconvenience sure but getting angry or upset at the inconvenience does what? Puts you in a bad mood. And your bad mood ripples out to those you come in contact with. Your work colleagues are going to just love being around you today... The more thought you give to a situation like this the more magnified the negative impact becomes.

Unfortunately, you can't control the boiler. I think I have met few people who do not have some kind of riveting boiler breaking story. But if you are one of the lucky ones... many other things break causing inconvenience, and you can't control this. What you can control (with some practice) is how you react to these situations.

You can lessen their impact by choosing to not let them affect you. I appreciate it may not always seem like you have a choice here in how you react but with practice it will feel more and more like you do.

The next time something like this happens consciously test out an alternative reaction of acceptance and productive action.

Ok the boiler is broken again. Take the productive action of calling the boiler repair company. Accept that maybe it will take a few tries, but it will get fixed eventually. Do not give it any more thought.

If you feel like it would help you to say this alternative reaction out loud then absolutely give that a go. This might make you feel like someone (albeit yourself) is giving you easy to follow instructions on how to cope so it can be useful. 'Ok the boiler is broken again. I will call the boiler repair company. I will not give it any more thought'.

Consider another example:

Laundry detergent you have used for years becomes discontinued so you are forced to change. This may not bother you in the slightest in which case you can skip over this paragraph and truly congratulate yourself for succeeding in being laid back about such things.

For many people, however, this can cause a lot of anxiety – 'why do they always have to change products that work perfectly well? If it was working for me surely it was working for many others? And it's been that way for years, why are they changing it now? Are they trying to cause me anxiety?? I'm now going to have to find a new one and maybe it will react badly with my skin or not smell very nice – this is a massive inconvenience!'

Well yes... it is a little on the inconvenient side, and bad skin reactions or smells you dislike may indeed arise from trying out new detergents but accepting this is out of your control will make things easier.

Instead of worrying about trying out something new, take productive action – read reviews, get friend's recommendations and then test some out. You may find a detergent you actually end up liking better than your original.

Acceptance is key – a product you like being discontinued is not something you can control. You cannot force the manufacturer to start producing it again. You could put together a petition to try and persuade them if you really felt that strongly but ultimately the existence of the product is out of your control.

What is within your control is your reaction to the situation and how you let it affect you. Look at it in a positive way and view it as a chance to find a new product that may clean your clothes better, smell nicer, be more cost effective etc.

Choosing to see it in a positive way will lessen your anxiety but this takes effort if your natural reaction is to experience anxiety. You have to make a conscious effort to notice the anxiety and counteract it with the positive view.

Happier thinking involves paying attention to your reactions, so you can consciously choose to change them if they are negative.

# Be kind

Carrying out acts of kindness for others makes the world a better place. Absolute fact.

Think of a time when someone has been kind to you - perhaps someone held a door open for you, let you go ahead of them in a queue, picked up something for you that you dropped, made you a cup of tea. Even just simply smiled at you.

Think how nice and thoughtful it was of them to do that and how it made you feel. Knowing someone has thought of you, even if in just a very small way, more than likely makes you feel happy. At least enough to raise a small smile, right?

So ok, you can't force others to be kind, but you are responsible for your own actions so being a kind person yourself is a good start to fostering kindness and a great feeling in itself.

Plus, it often produces a domino effect - kind acts make people happy and generally more likely to carry out kind acts themselves.

It may seem completely unrealistic to expect to change the whole world with your own increased kindness, but what is entirely realistic is the possibility that your own immediate world can change with your kind actions.

Being kind to others is definitely something I wish to promote but it's also important to include yourself when you are thinking about who you can be kind to.

To illustrate this, consider a scenario where you carry some plates to the table and drop one on the floor and it breaks.

Reaction choice one: 'Why was I not more careful? I'm so clumsy. I should have carried one at a time. I am always doing stuff like this. Why can't I do anything right...'

Reaction choice two: 'That's a shame but accidents happen. I will clear it up and not give it any more thought. My plate carrying skills do not require in-depth analysis.'

Neither of these two reactions is going to unbreak the plate but the second leads to much happier thinking. You could spend a long time ruminating with the first, wishing you had been more careful but a kinder reaction is to accept what happened and resist any urge to launch a highly unnecessary critical attack on yourself.

Dropping a plate is not a reflection on you as a person – we all drop things.

Consider another scenario - You do a presentation at work and it goes well for the most part, but you stumble over a few words and struggle to answer a couple of questions.

Reaction choice one: 'I am so bad at presentations. I will never get promoted. I might even lose my job. Why didn't I prepare more? I can't do this job.'

Reaction choice two: 'I am pleased that went well for the most part. I will research answers for the questions I struggled with so I can update people. I'm sure the more experience I gain the less I will stumble over words. No presentation is perfect.' You give it no more thought.

There are two main tips here when you catch yourself being unkind to yourself by reacting with the first reaction.

The first is to ask yourself how you would treat a good friend if it was them in the situation instead of you and then treat yourself the same. If a friend told you their presentation went badly you wouldn't say to them 'oh you must suck at your job, you'll probably get sacked' would you? (really hoping you answered no there...). You are your own friend so remind yourself of that in such situations.

The second tip is to give it no more thought. By all means assess the situation first – in the case of the presentation example it might be helpful to think about researching the questions you were unable to answer but once you've decided on actions such as those give it no more thought.

I appreciate this is way easier said than done sometimes, especially at first when you are re-training your brain to be kinder to yourself. You may find the unkind thoughts just keep on popping back up, taunting you like an annoying bully. But each time they do just notice them and remind yourself of the kinder alternative thoughts.

This can feel a little tedious and repetitive, but it becomes less so the more you practice. Over time the unkind thoughts will pop up less and less as your brain becomes more attune to the kind thoughts.

Happier thinking goes hand in hand with kindness. Kindness to all including yourself.

# Dwell on the good

You find out you failed an exam. One hour later you remember you failed the exam and feel your mood drop. This happens regularly throughout the day, so you frequently find yourself experiencing the same low mood.

The memory of the failed exam may not even have always appeared, but you went looking for it as you felt an unsettling feeling in your mind and knew something not great had happened. 'What was it? What happened today?' You start going over the events of the day until... ah yes... that was it. You've reminded yourself so now you get to feel the low mood again. Oh goody.

The next time this happens try a different approach – each time the memory of the failed exam pops up, consciously make an effort to dwell on something good.

Perhaps you had a fun night out, a success at work, went for a walk and caught a beautiful sunrise – pick something that will make you smile when you remember it. Then go into as much detail as you can think of for why it was good for you.

Practice doing this each time the failed exam memory appears, and this will likely lessen the low mood.

Bad things will still happen. I would love nothing more than to present you with ways to eliminate bad things in your life (annoying this book is not that I know - can someone please write that book?!). I can, however, provide suggestions for lessening the power of bad experiences on your mood. Counteracting the negative with thinking in great depth about something positive is a good strategy to try.

You might be in a situation where you go to work every day feeling like you hate your job. Everyone has days or even weeks when they dislike their job but if you notice you've been feeling this way for a while then stop and think about what action you can take.

Am I about to just tell you to get a new job? Groundbreaking advice there... jeez... did you pay money for this book?! Although the obvious advice would indeed be to look for a new job, and that is definitely something you should consider, it may not be so easy.

The job market may not be so great, or it may take time to find something new you think you will enjoy. There's no point leaping into the first new job you find as you don't want to end up just moving from one unhappy situation to another.

So, you may be stuck for a little while in your current job hating every day and in need of a way to cope.

Once you've realized you hate your job you will more than likely have stopped seeing any good in it at all because the hate has taken over.

Carry out a small exercise during your next work day and note down five good things about the job. This may seem impossible at first but tell yourself you are going to set aside the hate feeling for the day and make a real effort to notice some good.

Notice colleagues that you like. Notice nice lunch locations near your office. Notice skills you are learning. These may not be obvious skills – for example, are you dealing with difficult colleagues? This may be contributing to your hate of the job but look on it as a learning experience for developing skills on how to deal with difficult people. Your next job will have them too most likely I'm afraid... sorry... but you know I'm right... so why not test out approaches on dealing with them now so life will be easier for you in future similar scenarios.

Notice a nice view you might have out of your office window. Notice a good commute. What else, no matter how small, can you notice that's good?

These good things will not erase the bad but dwelling on them and bringing them to the forefront of your mind can make it much easier to cope with the bad feelings.

Often we only consider ourselves to be happy if the big things in life are going well for us – jobs, houses, relationships. There are so many other things that can make you feel happy though so try not overlook them.

It's important to note that it's not only when something bad happens when practicing this technique of dwelling on good will help. Do it when nothing bad has happened, or when nothing specifically good or bad has happened, at any time at all really... Occasionally and randomly pick times to practice the technique.

Do it when you are on your morning commute, when you are getting dressed, when you are preparing a meal, when the day has the letter 'u' in it – pick whenever works for you. This will begin training your mind to focus and really dedicate thoughts to good things.

I mentioned in an earlier chapter about how we often at the end of a day (or middle, or start, or let's face it, any part of the day really...) ruminate over something bad that's happened. Words like ruminate and dwell really just mean to think intensively about something, but they are most commonly associated with a bad something. Remind yourself they can be equally applied to good things and choose to practice them in that way.

Go into the detail of good things, don't just let them be passing thoughts. Reach out and hold the thought and examine why it's so good.

Happier thinking involves dedicating time to dwell and ruminate on good things.

# Act on what you can change

You are going on holiday today – woohoo! You really need this break and cannot wait to get away. You wake up on time despite it being the middle of the night. (It's pretty much mandatory for all the best holidays to start with a flight requiring you to get up in the middle of the night. It's just more exciting that way.) You gather up your suitcase, plane tickets, passport, and leave in a timely fashion for the airport. All good so far.

You get to the airport and smoothly navigate through the check in process. You get through security with little queueing and arrive in the departures lounge all ready to begin your travels.

You look up at the departures board scanning it for your flight. DELAYED. RED. CAPITAL. LETTERS. 'Noooooooo! This cannot be happening, this is my much needed, long overdue holiday, it has to go well! Why is the world against me??' Starting on this train of thinking is going nowhere good. By the end of it you could even have written off your whole holiday as a disaster – after all, it's started off badly now hasn't it? It's jinxed! You might as well go home.

Don't go home. Firstly, remind yourself of all the things that have actually gone well so far – getting up on time, smoothly getting to the airport, checking in and going through security etc. In the same way as an earlier chapter talks about not writing off the day, don't write off whole experiences like holidays based on one bad occurrence that might happen near the start.

The flight is delayed – you cannot change this, but you can change what you do next and how you react.

Option 1 – have a meltdown in thoughts as described above and believe all is bad and the holiday is doomed for disaster. Go and find a seat and ruminate negatively over these thoughts, continually checking the departure board for updates, getting irate at anyone and everyone who passes you.

Option 2 – accept delays occur and think of a plan for occupying your time until the new flight time. You could start reading a book you had planned to read on your break. Yes, I know, reading a book in an airport may not quite be the same relaxing experience as reading a book on a beautiful beach but once you become absorbed in reading you can absolutely still find enjoyment in it.

You could wander around the airport and browse in the shops. Sit in a cafe and use the time to think. Airports are generally filled with things for delayed passengers to occupy their time with so take the opportunity to appreciate the thought the airport planning people put into it. Everyone loves to be appreciated in their jobs and this is your chance to appreciate the airport planning people.

Getting irate and angry or down and depressed will not change the delayed flight. Looking for ways to occupy the time and accepting the delay as a small inconvenience will be a lot more productive in keeping your mind happy.

Consider another scenario – You enjoy your job and have been there for a while now. You've built up a good friendship with colleagues and feel like you are learning and growing in your role. One day you arrive in the morning and there is an ominous atmosphere. Not long after sitting at your desk you are called into a meeting. Your boss tells you that regretfully you and all your colleagues are going to be made redundant. The company office is closing.

Obviously this news is going to be upsetting and I am not going to suggest you dismiss and ignore those feelings and skip out the meeting with a big grin on your face, telling everyone to remember to still smile and be happy. 'Come on everyone, let's still think positive happy thoughts! Who wants tea?!' Those normally friendly colleagues may not be so friendly with you today...

This is quite a big event that warrants some unhappy feelings and I would not suggest you suppress such feelings.

But after a certain time you will want to move forward and try and pull yourself back to happier thoughts but this may prove difficult. You may be finding it difficult to accept what's happened as after all you loved that job. But accept it you must as you cannot change what has happened. It's out of your control. What you can do is act on other things that you can control.

You can start your new job search. You can work on your resume. You can apply for jobs. You can make contact with recruiters. You can get in touch with friends to see if anyone knows of any opportunities. You can brush up on interview skills.

These are all actions within your control to help you move forward and feel happier.

We generally feel better when we are doing something. Perhaps it's because it distracts us, or it makes us feel like we have some control. The reason is not so important – if being productive and taking some action makes you happier then it's a good strategy.

Happier thinking involves acting productively rather than thinking destructively.

# Don't compare your life to imagined others

Y ou're sitting on a train feeling negative and a bit low. Perhaps you're going through a rough time at the moment, you might be wishing you had a better job, a happy relationship, a child, better fashion sense... whatever it is, it's making you feel like you wish you had someone else's life.

You glance at the person sitting opposite you and notice they are attractive looking and are wearing nice clothes. You start thinking... The clothes look expensive, so they must be well off financially. They are wearing a wedding ring, so they must be happily married. They are attractive, so their life must be easy. You start wishing you were them. They must have a better life than you.

There are various reasons why this is unhelpful thinking:

- You are comparing yourself to an imaginary life, not the one that is actually in front of you. You have made a whole ton of assumptions that have created the imagined life. The reality of the person's life is almost certainly completely different.

- Bad things happen in everyone's life – no one is immune from this. Wishing you had someone else's life is just like wishing for a different set of problems. The person sitting opposite you on the train may be in an unhappy marriage. They could be struggling with a health issue. They might have just lost their job.

- Even if that person does have a good life right now, everyone's life has ups and downs so there would be no guarantee of happiness if somehow you could magically swap with them.

You might be thinking 'but I am not comparing my life to some stranger on a train, I'm comparing it to a friend and I know for a fact their life is perfect!'.

Well unfortunately that 'fact' is in fact highly unlikely to be true. No one's life is perfect. People often like to present their best selves to others, even to their good friends. It may appear perfection on the outside, but everyone goes through struggles.

Everyone wakes up looking less than attractive. Everyone has fashion disaster days. Everyone has health issues. Everyone has relationship struggles. Everyone has days when they hate their jobs.

All the energy you put into comparing lives and wishing for imaginary magical life swaps could be put to much better use. Use it to look for ways you could change your own life if there are specific things that are making you unhappy.

Happier thinking involves letting go of assumptions about other people's lives and not wishing away your own.

# Accept changed plans

Some of us like to plan our days and any deviation from those plans cause us great anxiety and negative thinking.

The problem here is that you can plan as much as you want, it won't change the fact that you will never have full control on how those plans will actually turn out. This means you are essentially setting yourself up for anxiety.

You might be saying – 'but I need to plan my days or how else will I get things done!?!' The suggestion here is not to do away with all your plans, rather to introduce acceptance into changes in those plans. You might now be saying - 'Oh excellent, that must mean I can create more plans to deal with every eventuality that may cause changes in my initial plans! Plans for changes in plans.' Er... not quite sorry... that is not the suggestion here. If making more plans was actually sounding like fun for you then sure, still go ahead but accept it will waste a lot of your time and ultimately unlikely still prevent you from being 100% prepared for every changed plan. But I'm not here to stop you having fun if planning makes you happy...

A different approach to lead you to happier thinking would be to simply practice the act of acceptance. I use the word practice here because if you are prone to getting stressed out about changed plans it's unlikely you will simply be able to switch that stress off the first time you try. Your natural instinct needs to be reset.

Each time you find yourself in a situation where your plans have been changed, try and allow yourself to just accept the situation rather than fighting against it by getting angry or annoyed or upset.

Another thing you can do is change the way you view your plans. Look on them as flexible or adaptable instead of being firmly set in stone.

Let's say your plan is this - After the plumber has come to fix the radiator I will go and pick up my prescription from the chemist. Plan sorted.

What actually happens is this - The plumber doesn't turn up and now the chemist is closed. Plan was a disaster.

If instead you changed your plan to - If the plumber arrives in time I will go and pick up my prescription from the chemist. You have made it flexible and less open to inducing stress.

Happier thinking involves accepting that plans are not definite things that will absolutely happen just because you have formed them in your mind or written them down in a neat little list on an orange post-it note. Resisting their changing nature is not going to change the fact they might change. (Perhaps over-use of the word 'change' there but I think it nicely emphasizes the fact that change happens a lot... like a big lot... so resistance is going to make life tough for you).

# Change path when it stops looking appealing

You are out for a walk somewhere you have not been before and the path you are on starts looking less and less like a footpath the further you walk. It becomes overgrown with foliage and less defined on the ground. It would make sense to not continue along this path since it's not providing a comfortable route for you to enjoy your walk. You change onto an alternative path.

Just as changing path is a good decision here, deciding when it would be good to change your path of thoughts is also useful. When a negative thought pops up in your mind this can often lead to further negative thoughts developing into a path of several negative unhelpful thoughts chaining one after the other, getting entwined with each other to make them more and more cumbersome. You don't need to keep following the path, you don't need to keep on introducing more negative thoughts, there are other paths your brain could take.

The next time you feel yourself following a negative path with your thoughts, make a conscious effort to choose a different path. Think of something else that is unrelated to your bad path thoughts. Then follow the new train of thinking to lead you onto the different path.

You might find you are regularly drawn back to the negative path, for some reason it is enticing, but just take the same action each time this happens – think of the unrelated thought to pull you back again on to the alternative path.

This can often feel like quite a struggle. It feels easier to give in and just accept getting down and dirty with the foliage. If it helps you could look on it as though there is a person at the end of each path.

The one at the end of the negative thinking path is someone you are not so keen on – maybe someone who bullied you at school, or a work colleague who gives you a hard time.

The person at the end of the positive thinking path is someone you very much like. A friend, a loved one, someone you look forward to spending time with.

Each time the negative path person tries to engage with you, politely acknowledge them with a smile or wave (you are a nice person after all, so you would of course be polite...) but make no effort to move towards them. Instead you want to focus your effort on going to the positive thinking path person because you know their company is far preferable.

Happier thinking involves challenging your thought path. Remind yourself that there is an alternative more appealing path you could take if you search for it.

# Don't make assumptions

How often do you hear the advice that you shouldn't care about what other people think? Whilst that may be true in theory, in reality most of us seem unable to help ourselves from caring very much.

One problem with this is that you can never truly know for sure another person's thoughts. They might come right out and tell you what they are thinking, but even then, this is not a 100% true representation since they could be embellishing, leaving certain things out, or just plain lying.

Our mind can often get carried away with making lots of assumptions about other people's thoughts and in turn it allows those assumptions to affect us.

Let's really think about what's going on here – assumptions are not reality so if we get depressed because we assume someone is thinking badly of us we are essentially getting depressed about an imaginary situation. Something that may or may not be true.

I could reinforce the advice here to just not care about what other people think but personally I find that a pretty difficult thing to do and in many instances I actually do care what others think - yes they are mainly friends and family but they are still 'other people'.

So instead I will offer this advice - the next time you catch yourself making an assumption about someone else's thoughts, question your assumption. Ask yourself if it's possible they might be thinking something else entirely. Try and think of more than one alternative thought they could be having to challenge your assumption.

It is of course possible that your initial assumption was correct but is it not kinder to yourself to switch your assumption to one of the nicer alternative options? Let's consider an example...

You receive negative feedback from a colleague on a piece of work you've done. The thoughts that enter your head are... Oh gosh, they must think you are terrible at your job. They are probably wondering how you even got the job in the first place. They are currently chatting with another colleague and have just looked in your direction – they must be discussing how rubbish your work was.

There are many assumptions you are making here:

- Your colleague is judging your overall ability to do your job based on one piece of work

- Your colleague didn't see any good in your work at all

- Your colleague is discussing you negatively with others in a conversation you cannot hear

- Your colleague thought more about you beyond assessing that piece of work

The reality could just as easily be that your colleague thought your work was good overall but found one thing that could be improved on so fed this back to you and then they gave you and your work no more thought. They are currently chatting with the other colleague about the latest episode of a show on Netflix/Amazon/other streaming service, and only looked over in your direction because you sit next to the window and they were curious about the current weather situation...

Consider another example – You have arranged to meet a friend for dinner and they end up cancelling. The thoughts that enter your head are... Oh they must not have really wanted to meet you, they got a better offer, they can't consider you that good a friend if you are easy to cancel on. Thinking about it, it's always you that arranges the plans for meeting when you do meet up.

The reality could be that they had been really looking forward to meeting but something completely unavoidable came up that prevented them from going. They are feeling very disappointed as they always enjoy your company. They are actually aware you always make the arrangements and are very grateful for your organizing skills because they know their own are somewhat lacking. Some of us are event organizers, others are attenders, it doesn't translate that one is necessarily more willing to be there than the other.

The initial assumptions you make are indeed all viable but equally possible are alternatives as shown in the above examples. So if you can't know which are the truth then be kinder to yourself and choose to believe the nicer version. Or at least be open to the fact that alternatives exist.

Happier thinking means opening your mind to the possibility of alternatives and not accepting all your assumptions as truth.

# Question your thoughts

If you consider yourself a worrier, then I suspect you feel pretty exhausted a lot of the time. Worrying takes up a lot of energy and is more often than not simply wasted energy.

This is a pretty hard thing to change but something you can try is to spend some time really examining what it is you are worrying about. Ask yourself some questions:

What is the real cause of the worry?

Is this something serious?

Is it something important that requires a lot of thought?

Is it helpful or unhelpful to think and worry about?

In some instances your answers may well confirm and justify the worry but in many others they may make you realize the lack of point or need to worry, and therefore make it easier to stop.

Let's look at some examples.

You are worried about waking up late and not getting to work in time for an important meeting.

Is this helpful or unhelpful? Probably unhelpful as worrying keeps you awake and more likely to sleep through your alarm when you eventually do fall asleep.

Is it an important thing to worry about? You obviously don't want to be late for your meeting so it's not entirely not important but it's not something that requires a lot of thinking. You need only think about what actions you can take to prepare. Setting your alarm at the correct time, and possibly preparing anything you need for the morning to make it easier and quicker to get ready. Once that is done is there more thought required that worrying heaps on? Probably not.

Another example...

You are worried about something that might happen in the future but equally might not happen.

This is a pretty vague one I know but the principals can apply to many things covered by this general common worry.

Is this helpful or unhelpful? Worrying about something that might not even happen is similar to the earlier discussed process of comparing yourself to an imaginary life. It's worrying about something that is not real, therefore, a waste of your worrying energy.

You worry because you didn't have time to clean up the kitchen before you left for work and it's a bit of a mess.

Is this something serious to worry about? No. I'm not advocating that we all live in squalor and all cleaning chores should be abandoned since they cause us unhappy thinking. But worrying about a small bit of uncleanliness in your home is not a serious thing to worry about.

Happier thinking involves questioning your thoughts. Don't just accept and suffer in your worrying. Question whether it's helpful and a serious thing to worry about. The questioning process will hopefully make you realize if it's really worth continuing on with dedicating all that energy to worrying.

# Final thoughts

An important thing to remember that is relevant throughout all the chapters in this book is the word awareness. If you finish this book and that one word is all that you remember, then it will still be a worthwhile read. Well... as long as you remember what the word awareness relates to... So maybe slightly more than just one word for the worthwhileness but you get the point.

Awareness of how you are currently thinking. You need to notice what your current thoughts are in order to challenge and change them. Coasting along on autopilot thinking will not give you the opportunity to change anything.

Psychologists will tell you that thoughts are just thoughts, they are not reality. Thinking on autopilot often leads to just assuming all your thoughts are reality.

Reducing negative thoughts therefore requires turning off the autopilot and thinking about the thought. Focus on it and challenge it to steer yourself away from negative to positive.

I truly hope you find this book useful and gain some benefit from it but if you don't then I would urge you to try others. There is so much great advice out there, people sharing their own experiences and suggestions.

There is not one formula that will work perfectly and exactly in the same way for all of us unfortunately. It's kind of like exercises you do to keep the rest of your body healthy in that there are many different types - gym workouts, cycling, swimming, walking, running etc. etc. It can take a little while to figure out which one is going to suit you best. (I think I'm still in that figuring out process for my enjoyable physical exercise but I'm sure it is out there somewhere... somewhere quite well hidden).

In a similar sense there are many different exercises you can do to keep your mind healthy and happy, and this book is a collection of just a few options to try.

There are many more of these options in existence so if you found this book a bit useless then please do keep an open mind about others and keep searching for what works for you. If you did find it useless you possibly already gave up reading a while ago in which case this paragraph is a tad redundant... but I'll leave it in just in case, and as a note to the other readers for encouragement to keep searching out other options to build your own collections of what works for you personally.

I would also like to point out that I do think it's perfectly ok to just feel sad sometimes. I don't start manically scrambling for an exercise every single time I feel unhappy about something. Sometimes just experiencing the sadness is perfectly acceptable and a process you have to go through. That's why I named this book 'Happier Thinking' and not 'Happy Thinking At All Times. No Sadness Ever'. Life involves experiencing all emotions but the options in this book can help you cope with the less happy emotions and make them fewer.

Each day we are faced with situations that will challenge our happiness. Very small things, very big things, very medium things... regardless of the size or what affects you specifically, I truly wish you well in training your mind to achieve happier thinking.

It can be done. Just keep trying.

If you would like to get in touch with questions, comments, or just to say hello, I would love to hear from you – either visit my website:

http://lanagraceriva.com

Or email:

lana@lanagraceriva.com

# Reminders

*Don't write off the day*

*Turn negatives into positives*

*Journal good things*

*Much you can't control but your
reactions you can*

*Be kind*

*Dwell on the good*

*Act on what you can change*

*Don't compare your life to
imagined others*

*Accept changed plans*

*Change path when it stops looking
appealing*

*Don't make assumptions*

*Question your thoughts*

29278711R00032

Printed in Great Britain
by Amazon